The ABC's of Hotpot

By Venith Chance

A is for appetite!

As we begin,
let's do this right!
First you'll need
a big Appetite!

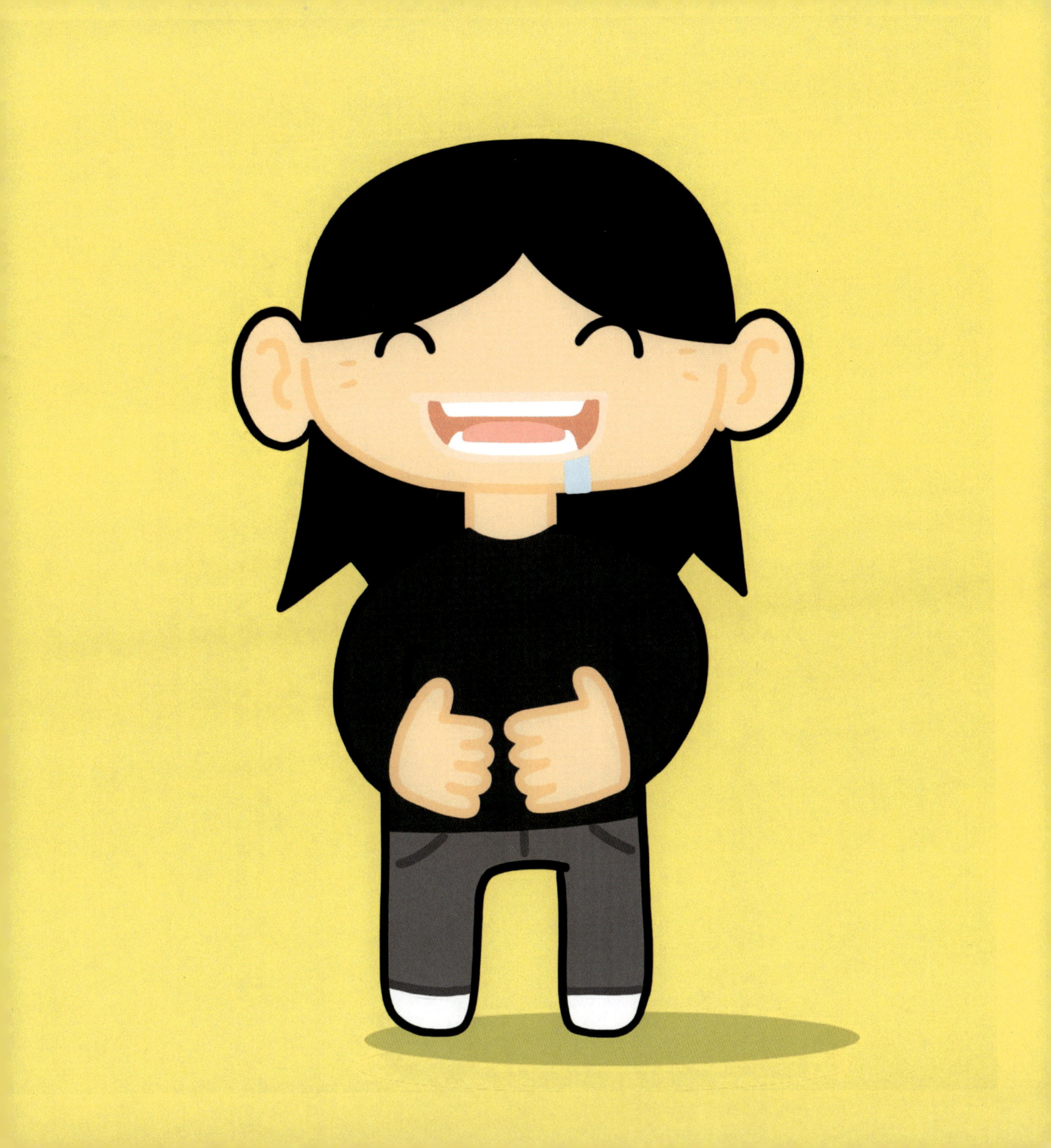

B is for base!

Light, strong
or a spicey taste?
You'll need to know
for your soup **Base!**

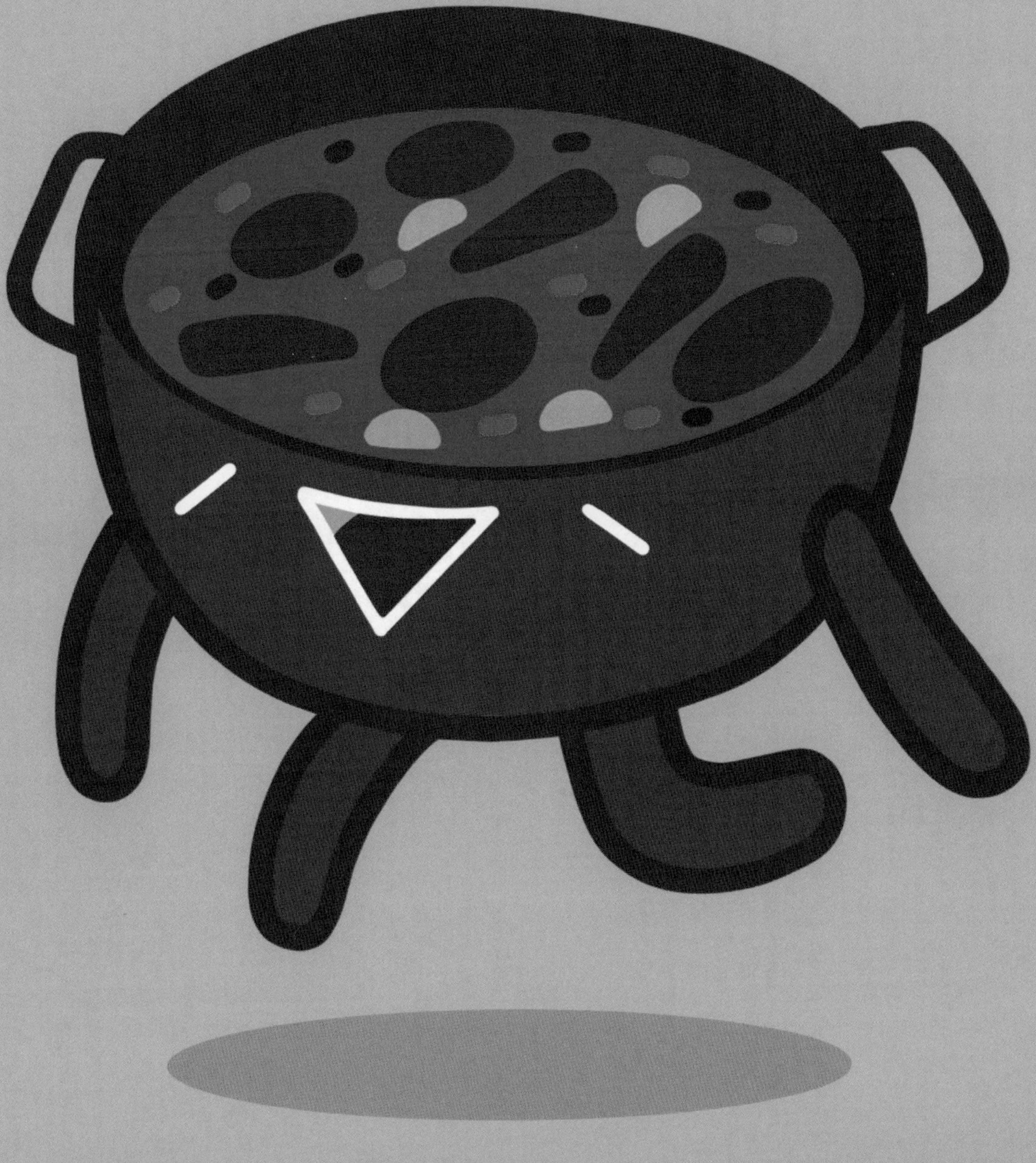

C is for choi!

Choi Sum!
Bok Choi!
Nappa Cabbage!
Leafy Greens
push out the
baggage!

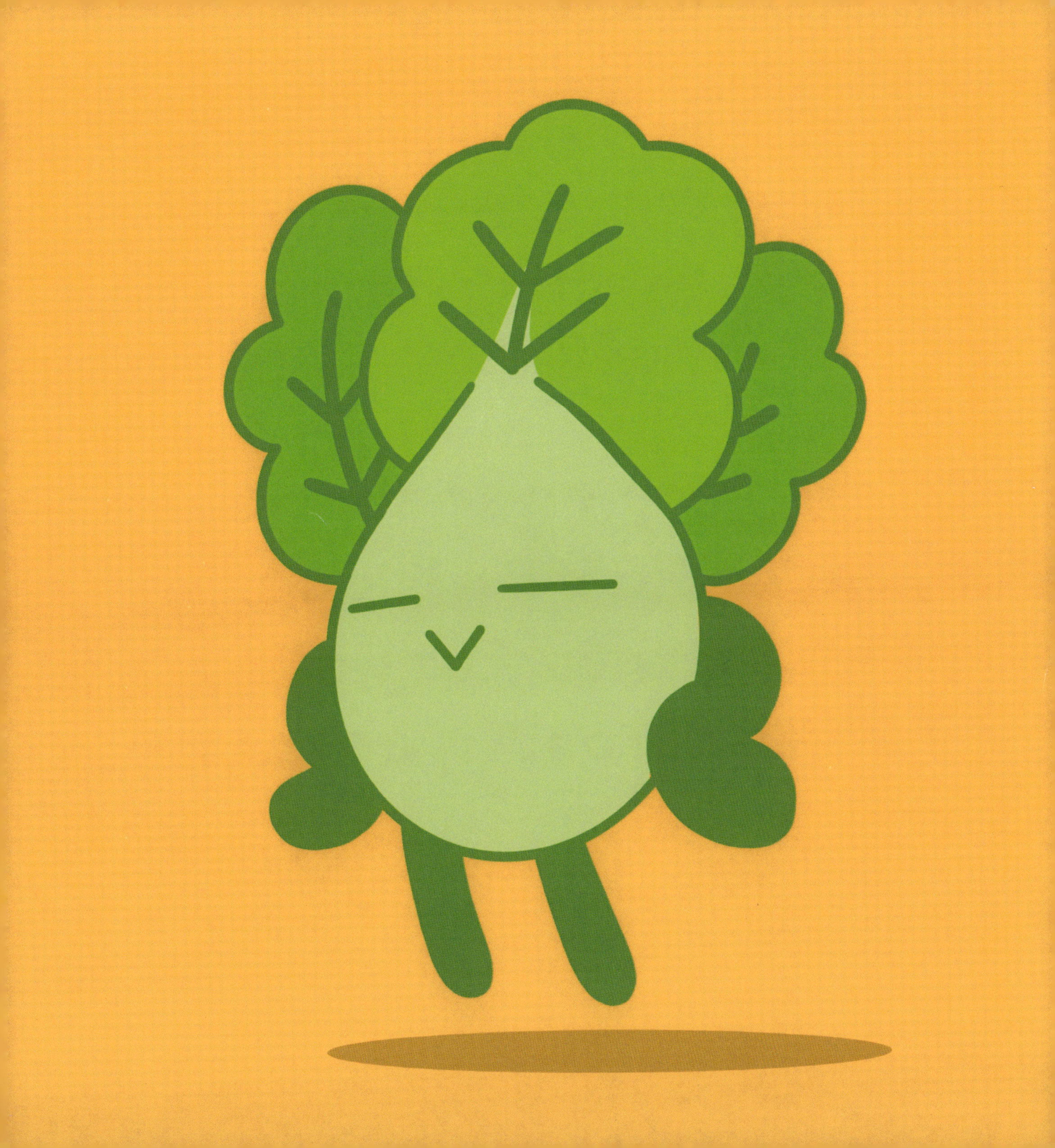

D is for dipping sauce!

Your tastebuds would be at loss, if you forgot the Dipping sauce!

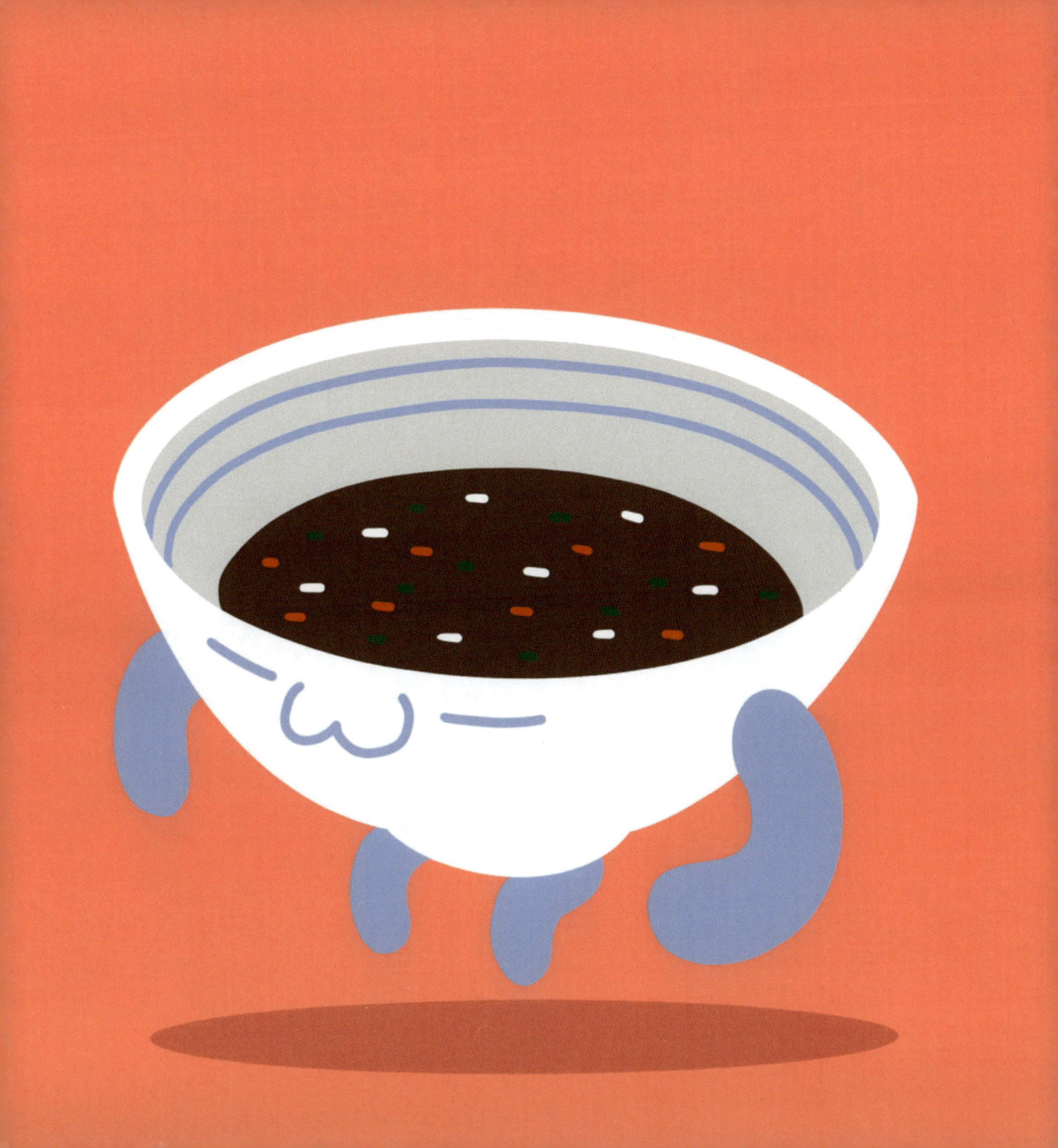

E is for enoki!

Addressing the elephant in the room: The rhyme stinks for *Enoki* mushroom!

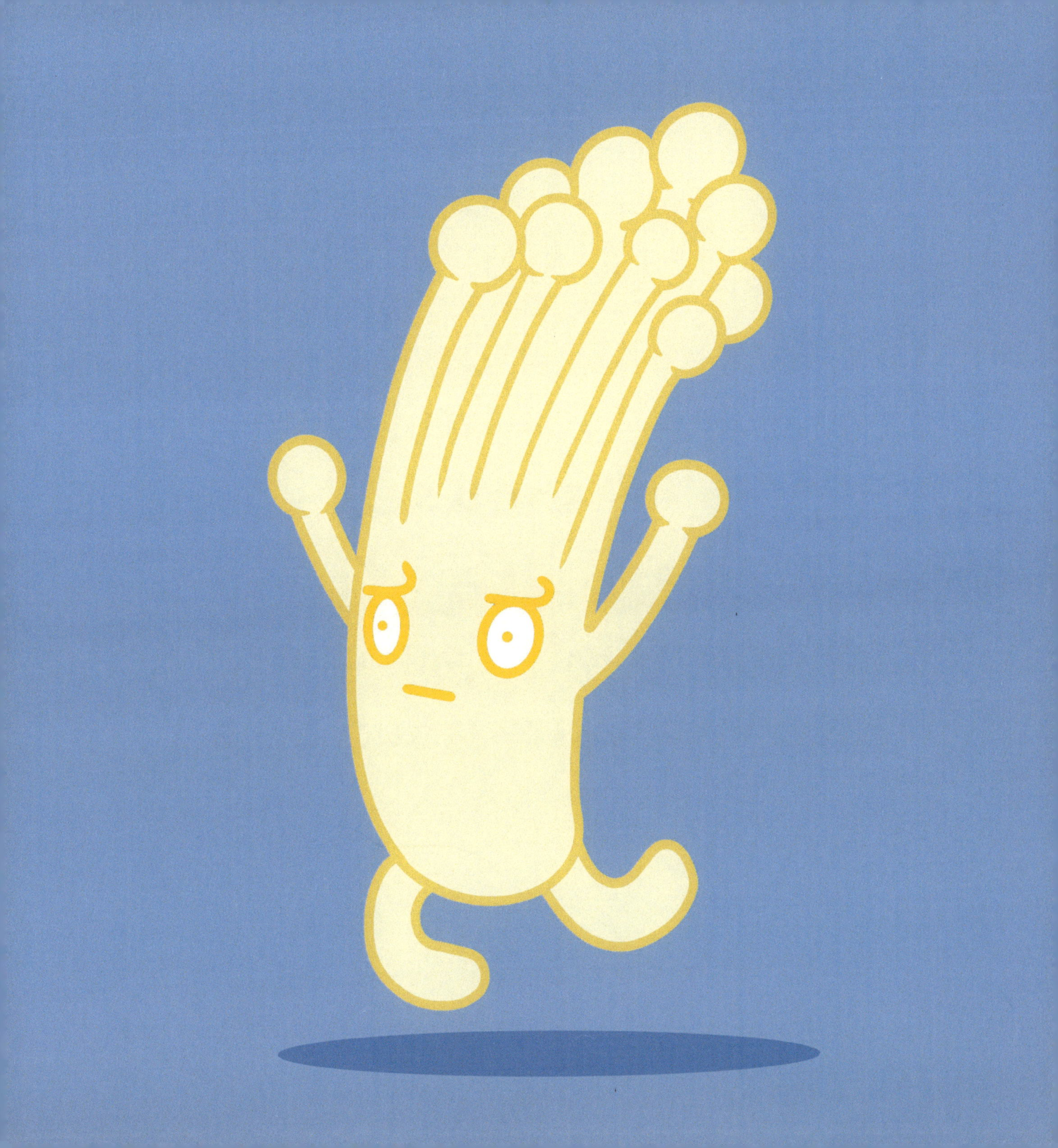

F is for fish!

Fishball,
Fishcake,
Fish Fillet!
Essential ingredients
to impress your bae!

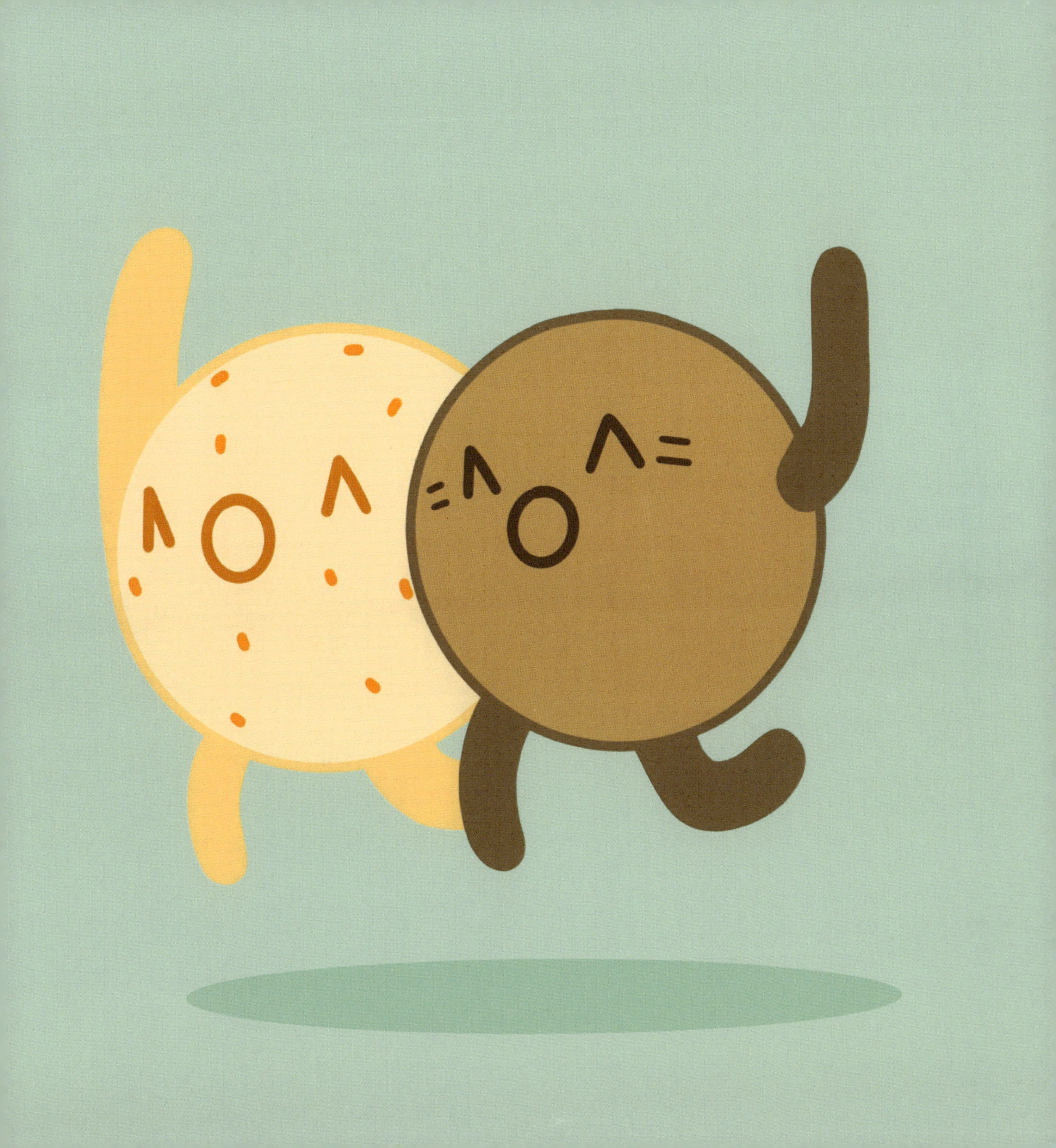

G is for garlic!

Vampires hate it,
it makes them sick
But I can't live
without Garlic!

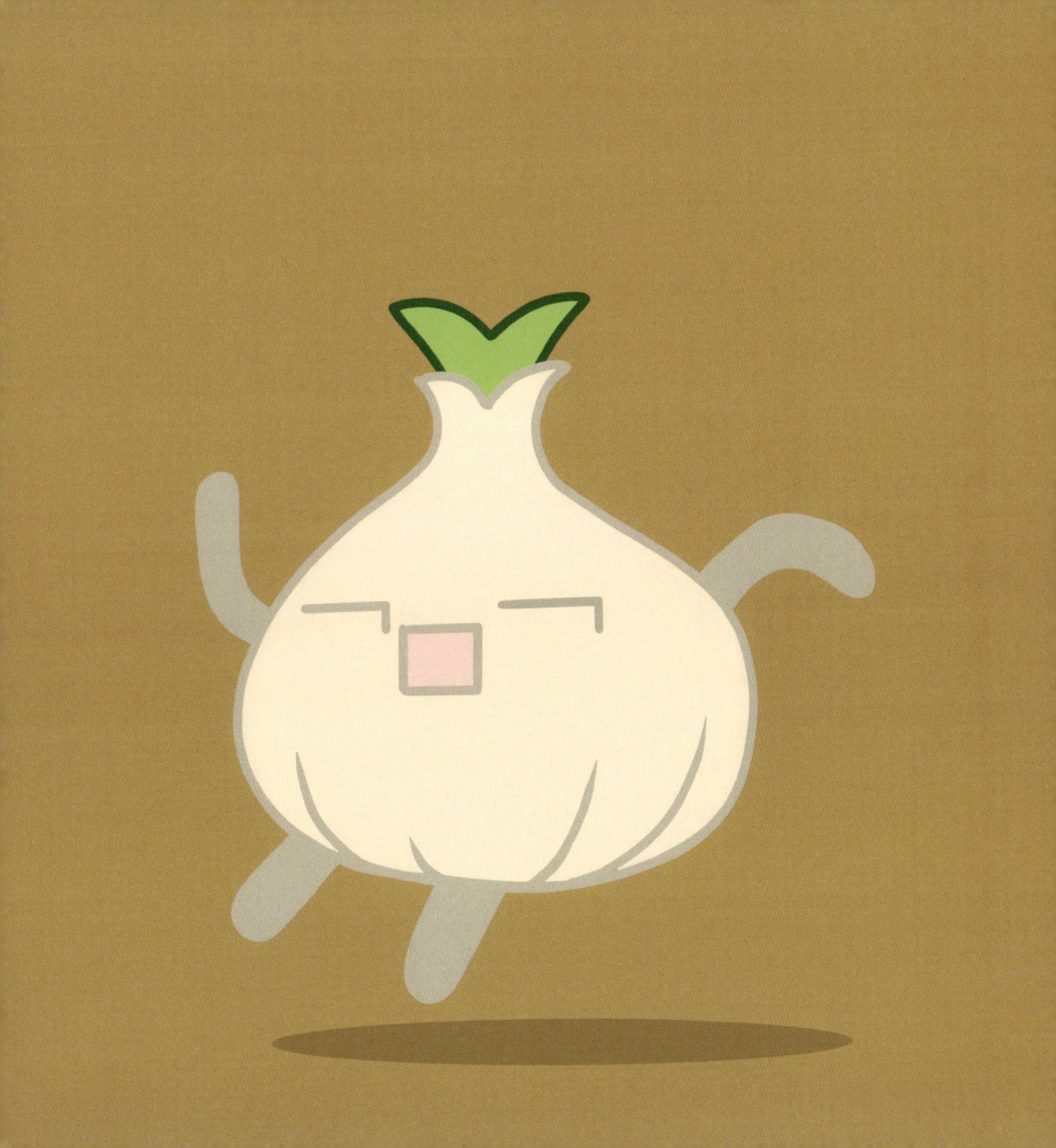

H is for hotdog!

If you seek beauty,
may I suggest Prague!
If you seek flavour,
may I suggest hotdog!

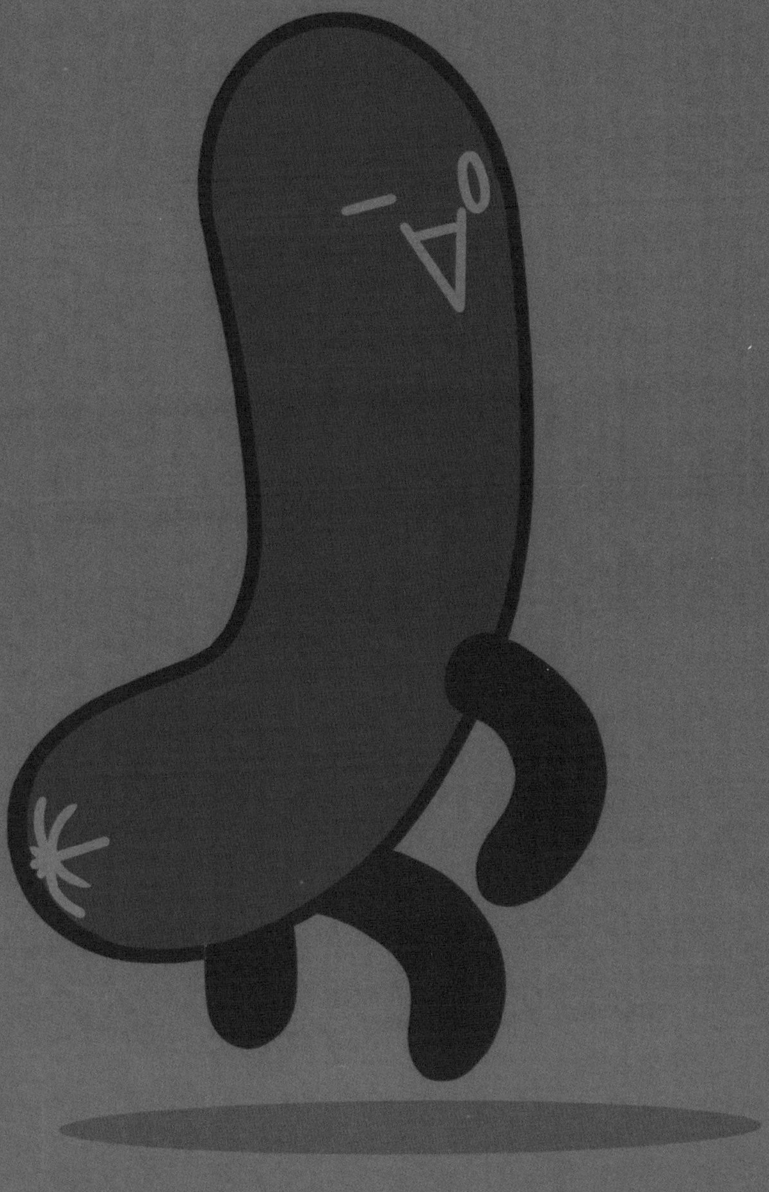

I is for iceberg!

Flavour tours,
hop on the bus!
Our first stop,
iceberg lettuce!

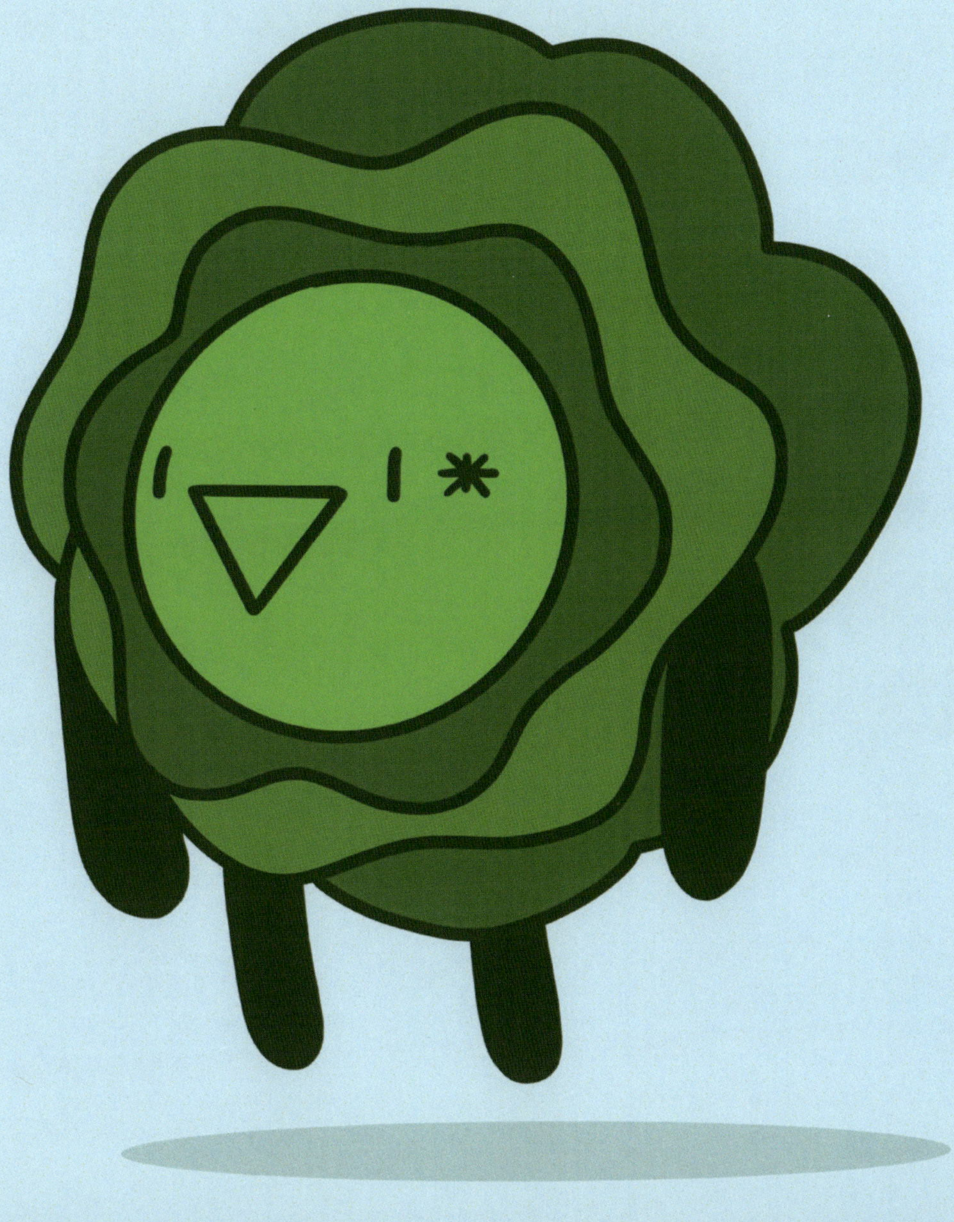

J is for Jiaozi!

I love you,
"wo ai ni"!
I love dumplings,
"wo ai Jiaozi"!

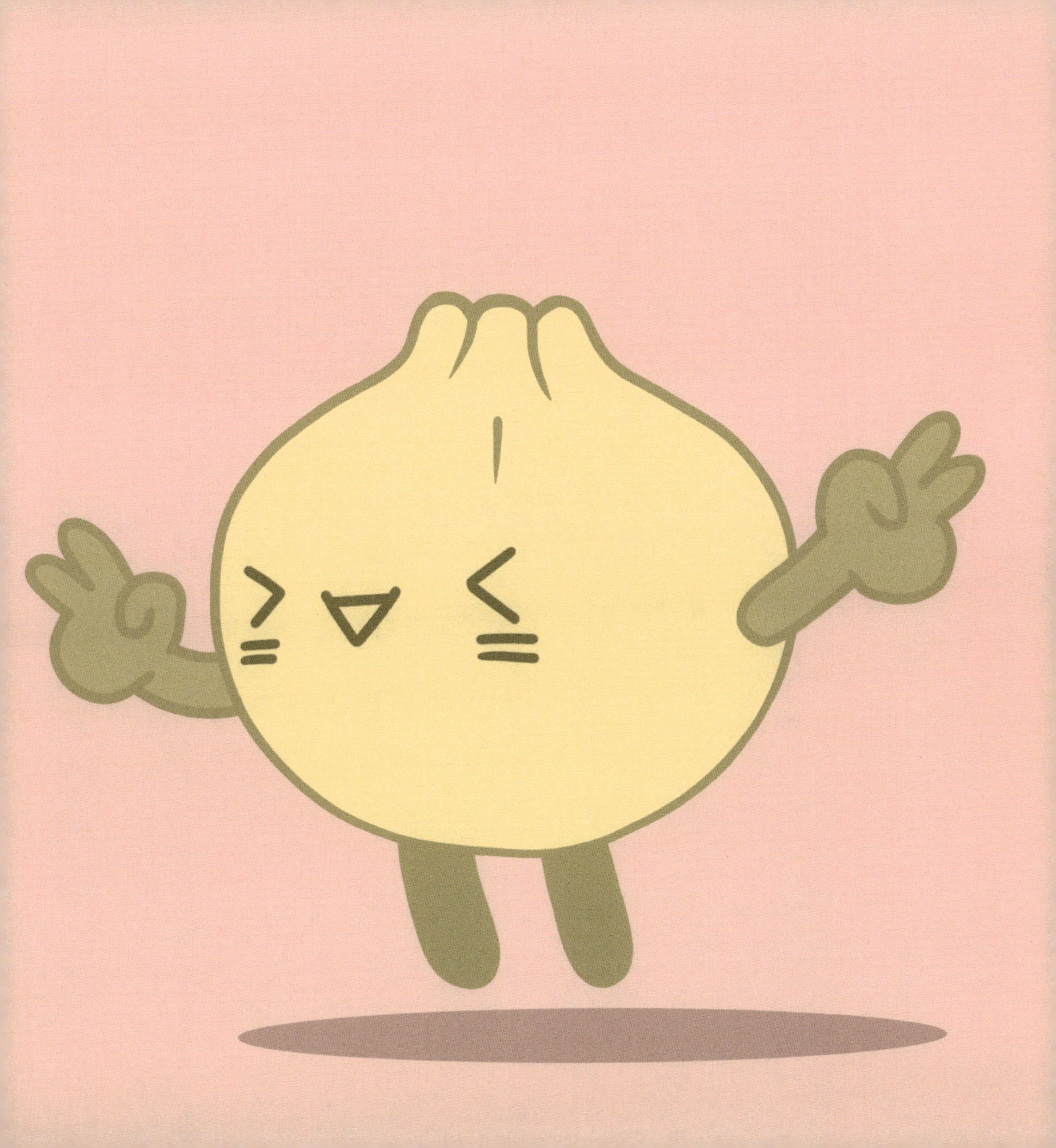

K is for King!

All hail!!
Royalty in the room!
All bow down
to King Mushroom!

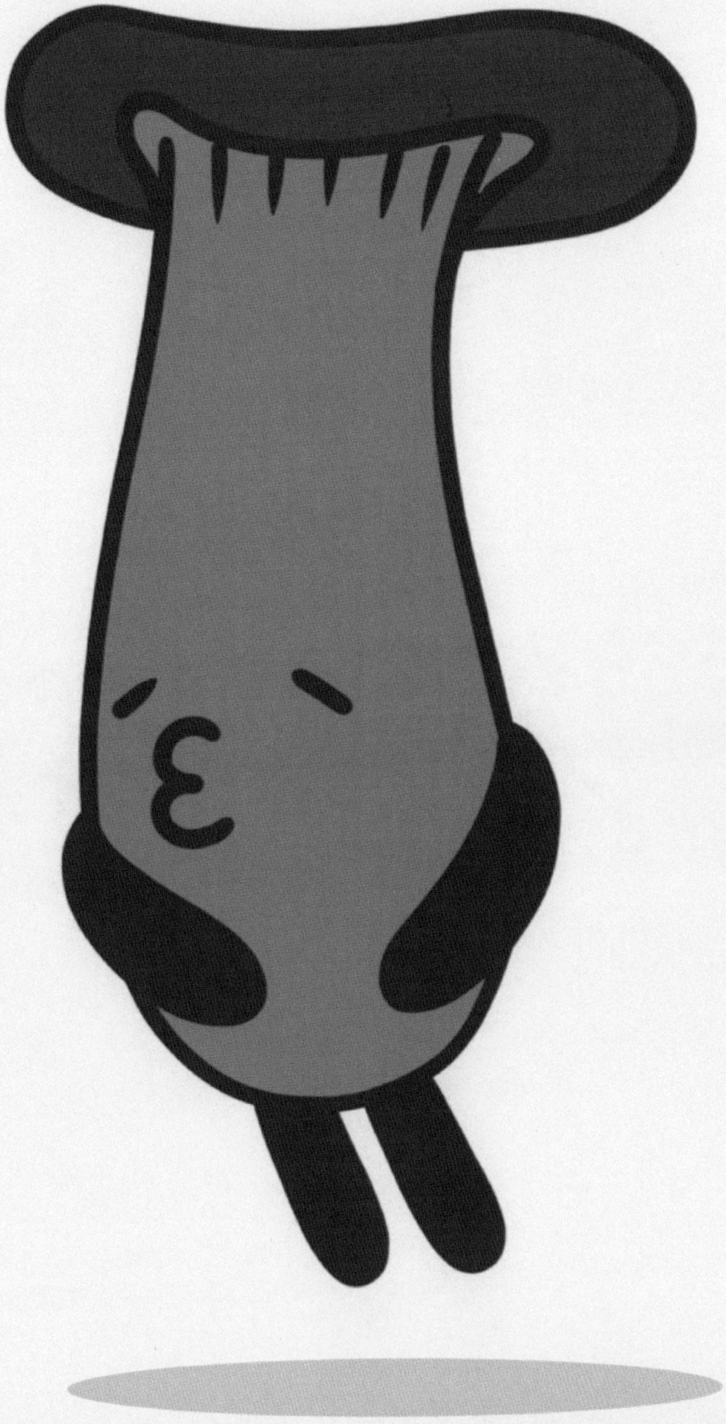

L is for lotus!

Way to go!!
woot! woot! woot!
You can do it,
Lotus Root!

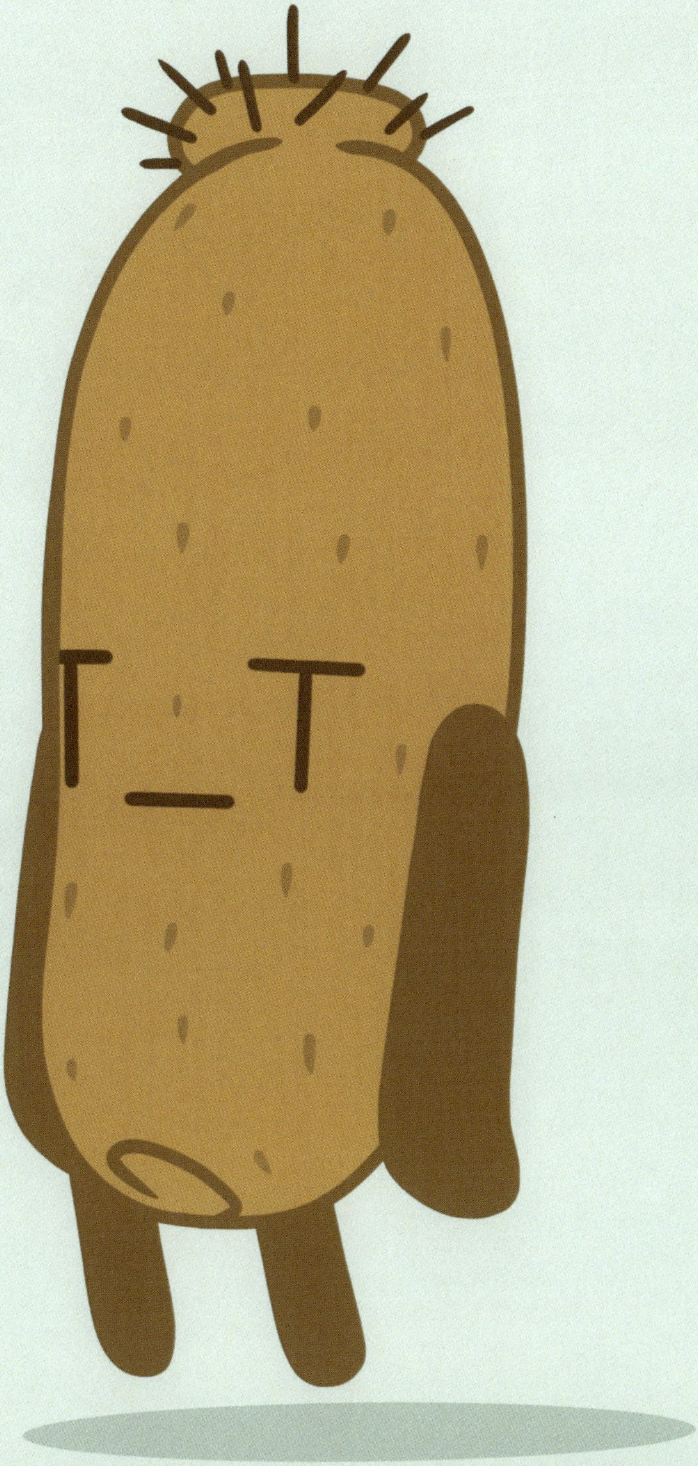

M is for meat!

Beef!
Pork!
Lamb sliced meat!
Without this,
hotpot is incomplete!

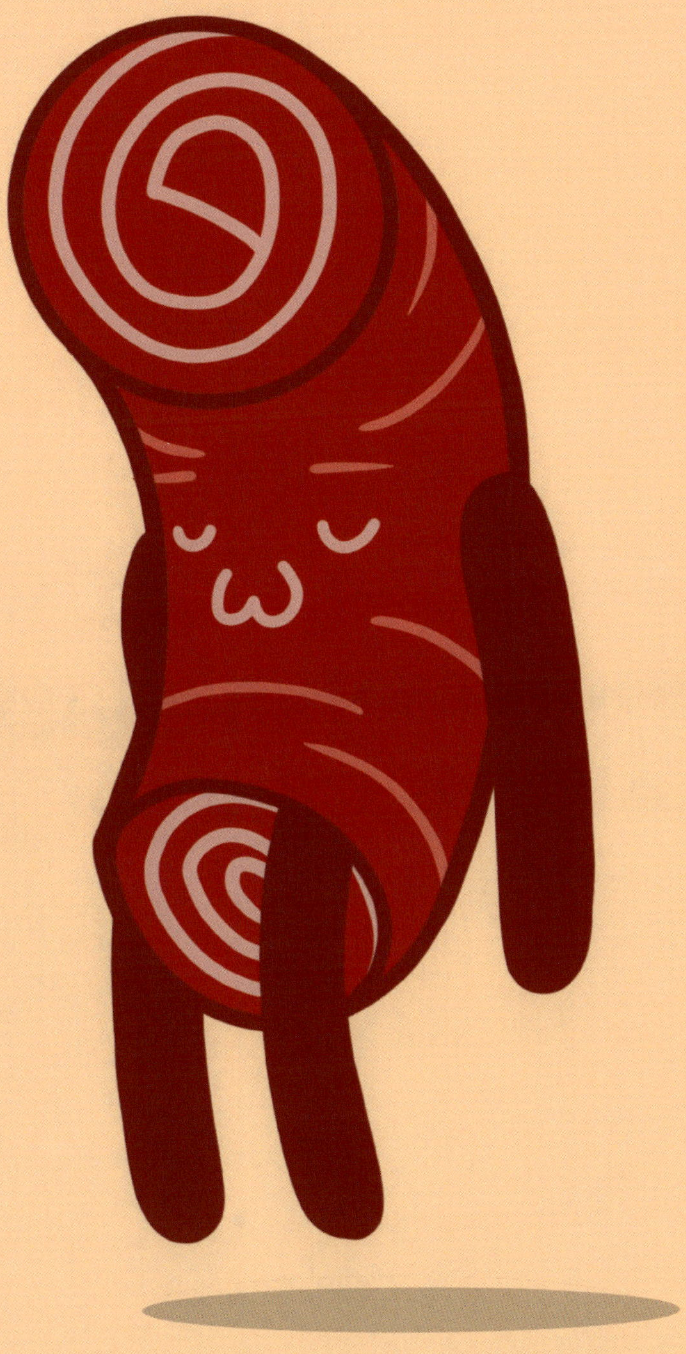

N is for noodle!

The honest truth
can be brutal!
But we all know
rice is second to noodle!

O is for oyster!

Professional tip to become the boss! Replace your perfume with oyster sauce!

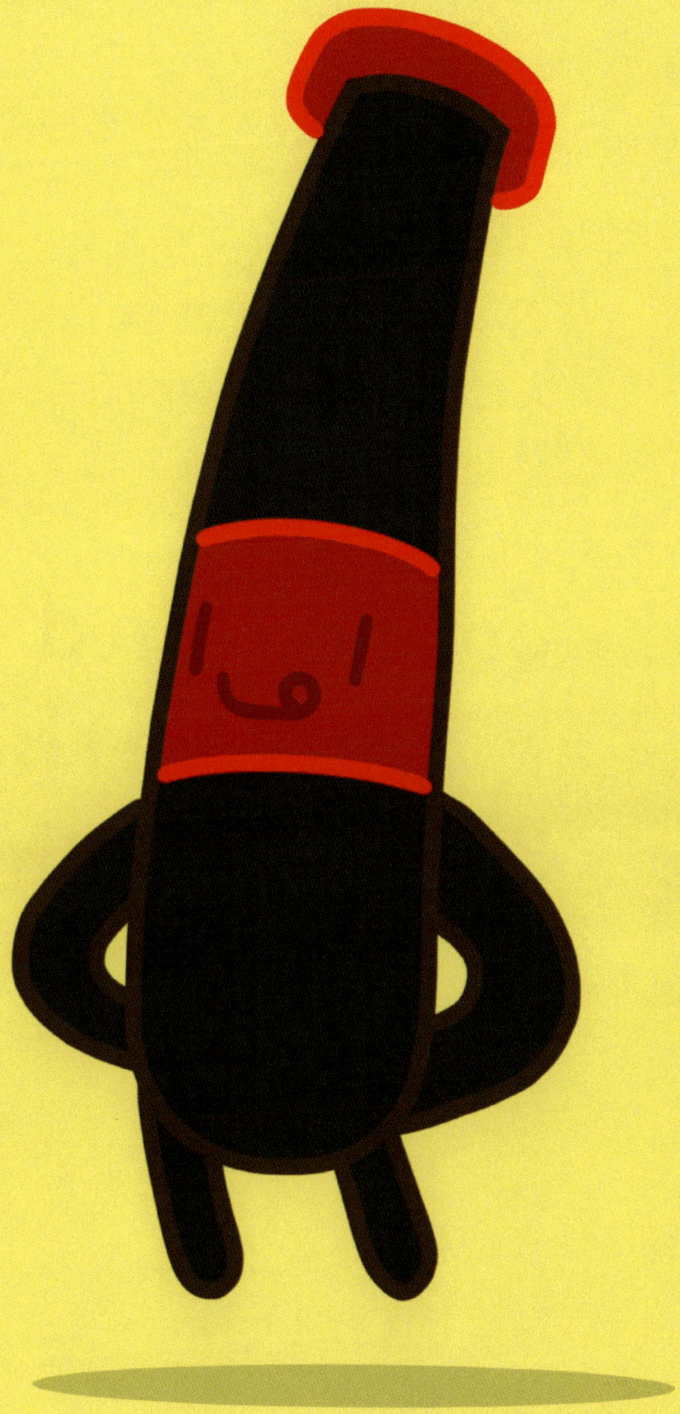

P is for peanut butter!

Mom and dad
sister and brother,
we stick together
like Peanut Butter!

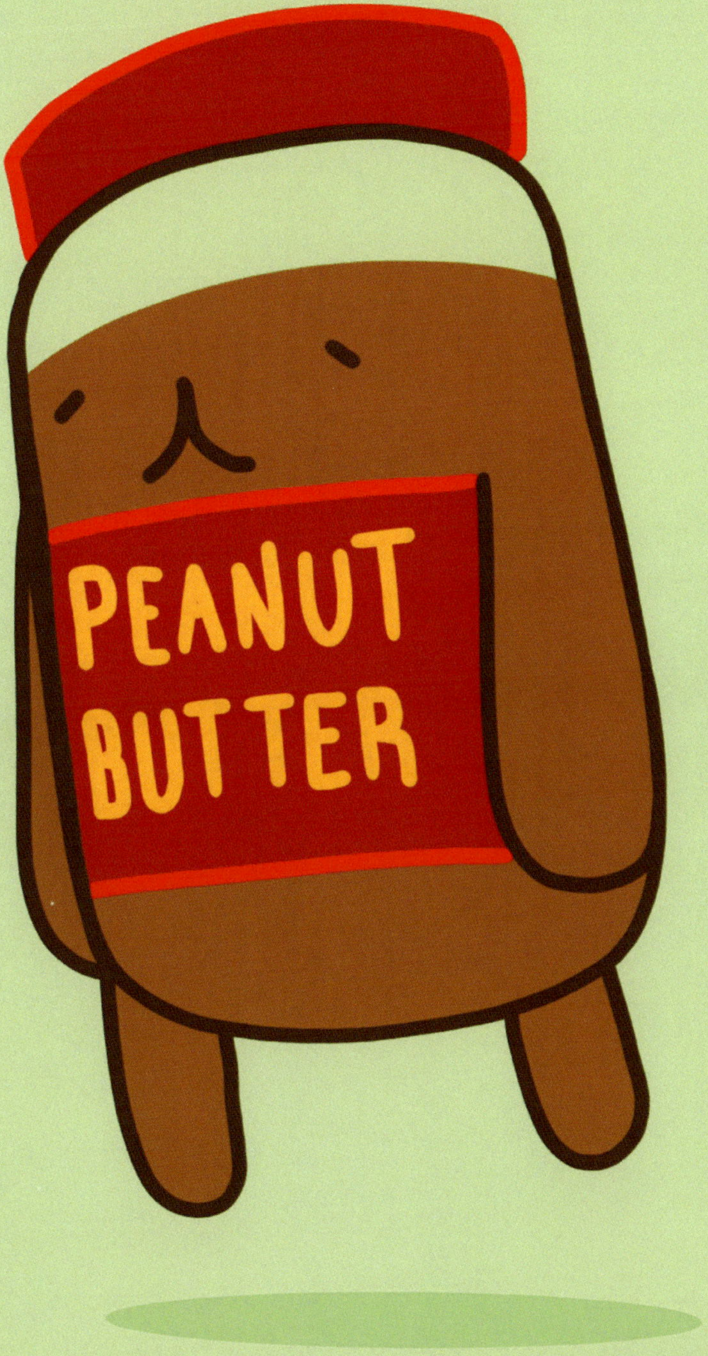
PEANUT
BUTTER

Q is for quail!

Don't judge an egg simply by scale!
Or you will miss the best from quail!

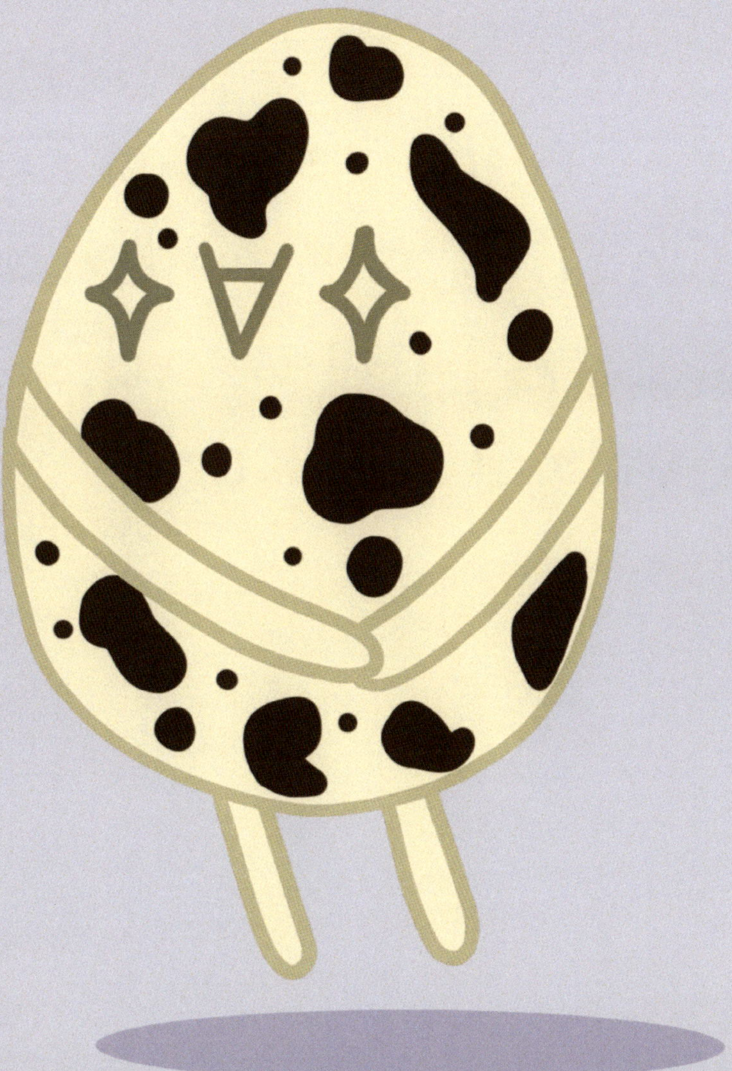

R is for Radish!

A little mad?
Then you're maddish!
A little rad?
You're a Daikon Radish!

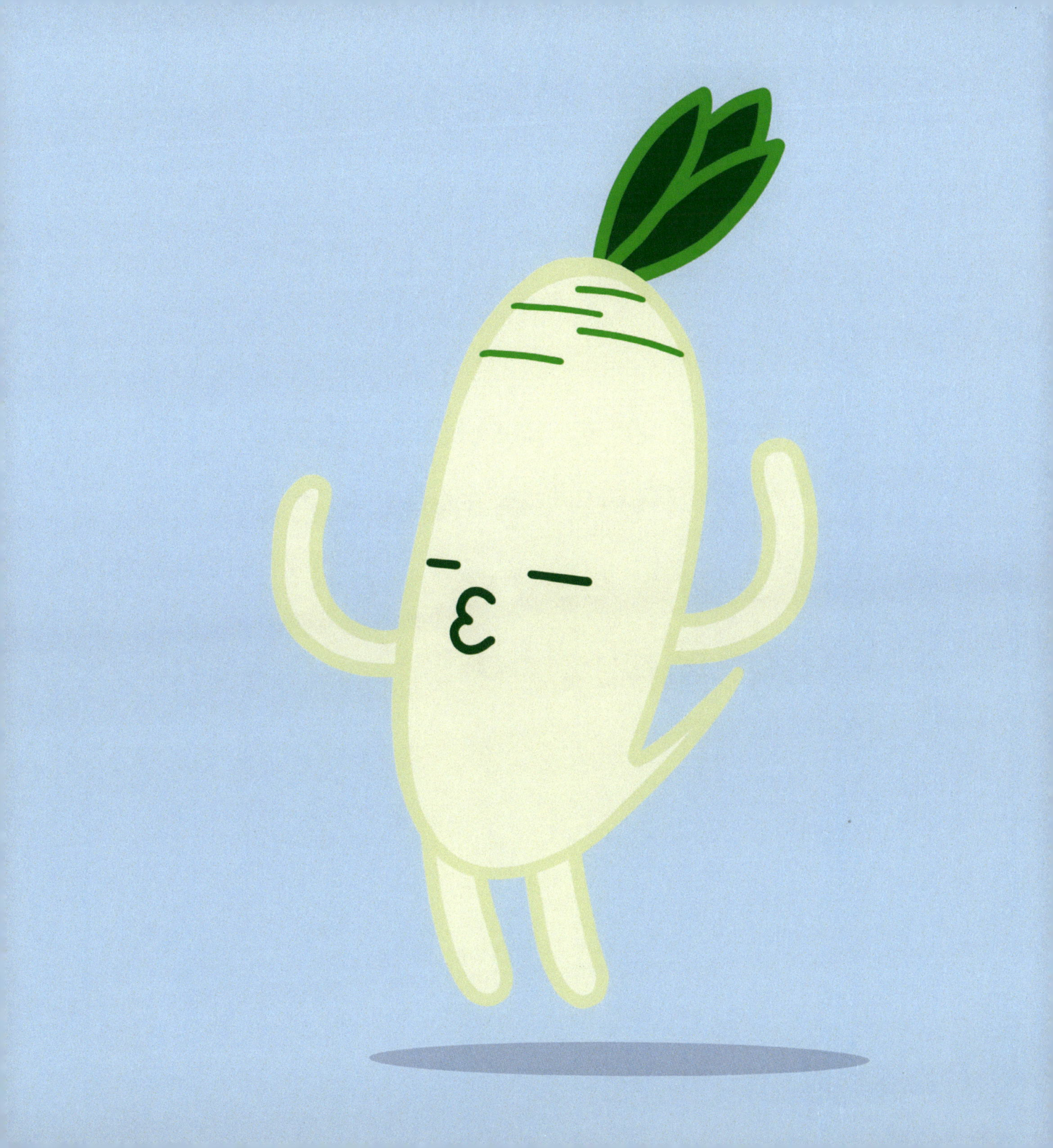

S is for spinach!

Let me paint you
a funny image,
me eating all
your delicious Spinach!

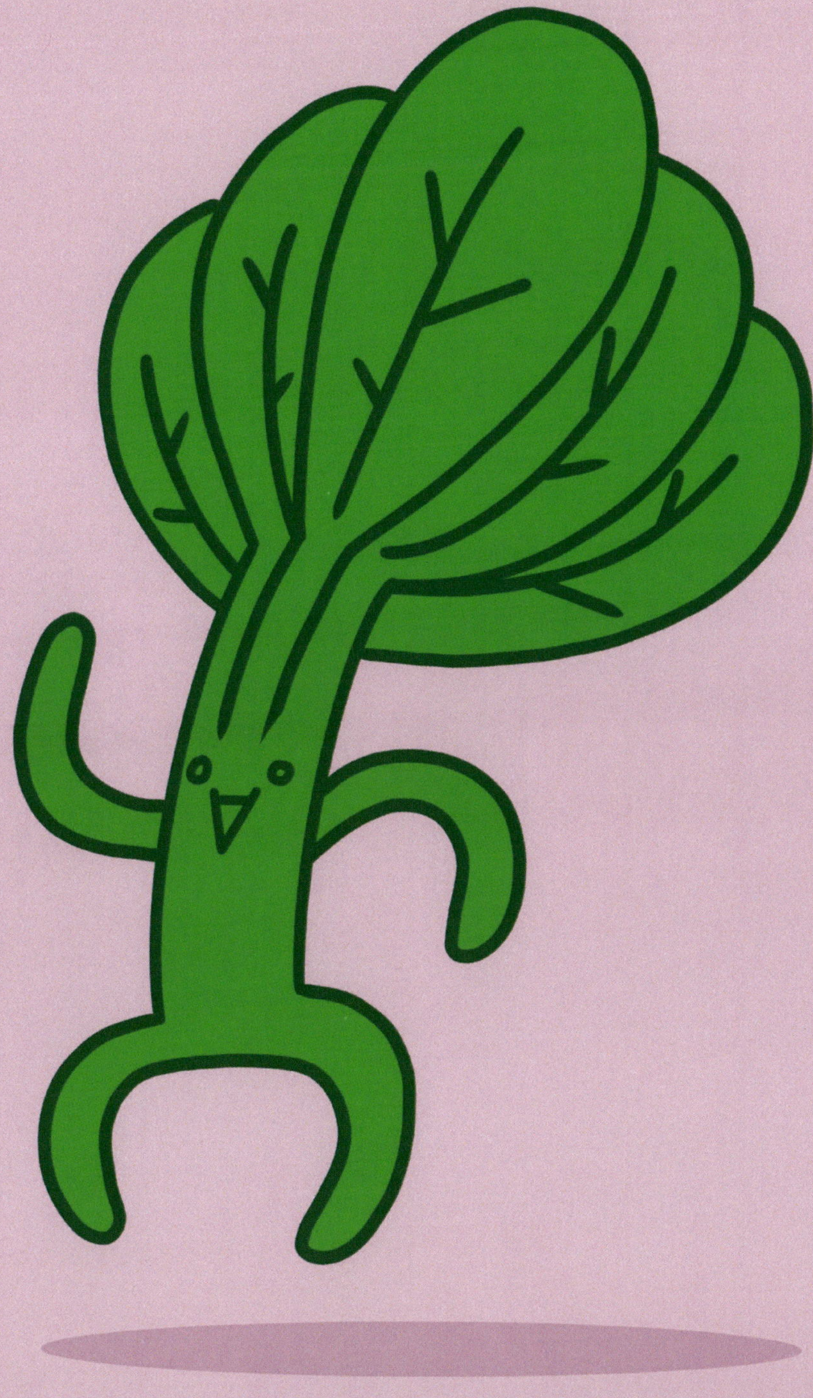

T is for tofu!

You are what you eat?
Let me show you!
My belly is soft
just like Tofu!

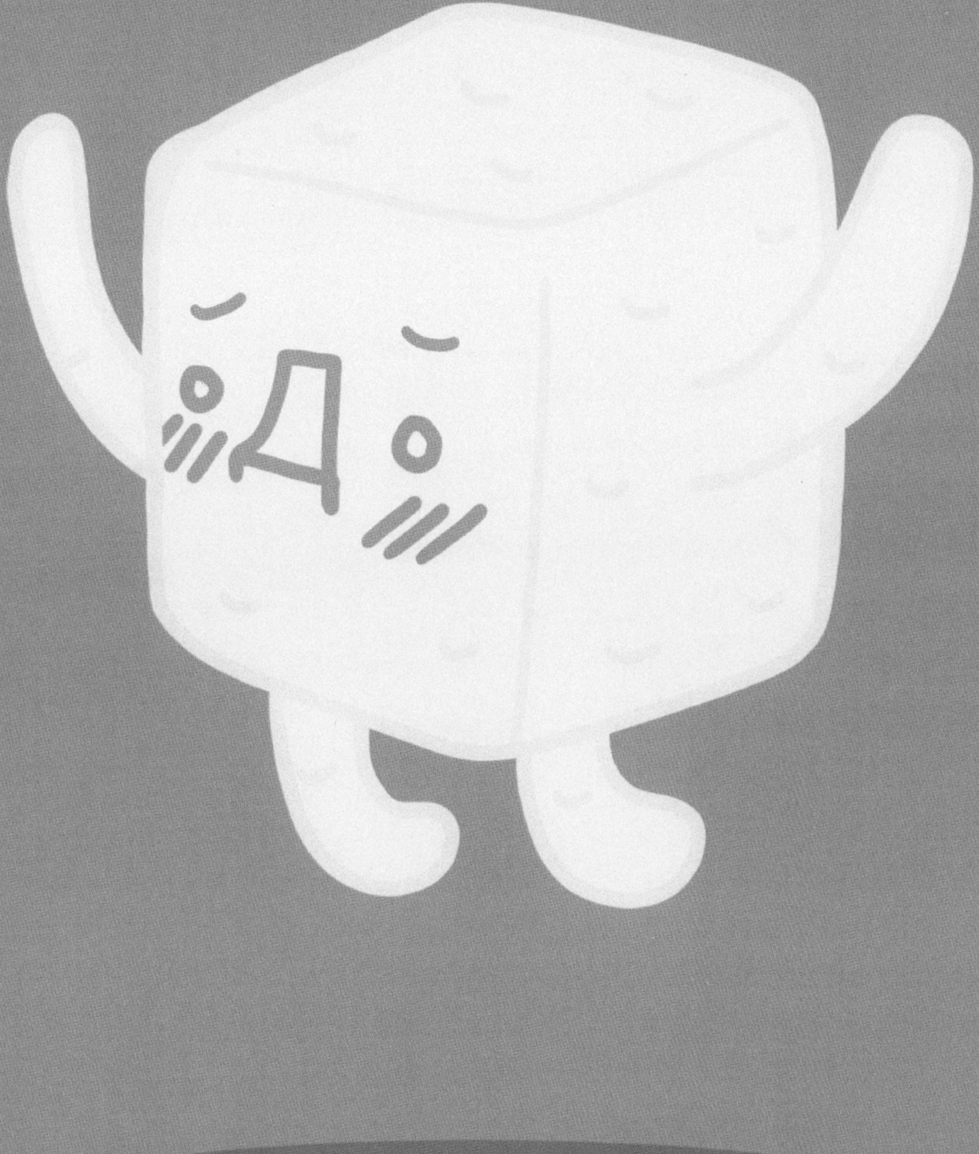

U is for udon!

Yellowknife
is found in Yukon!
Flavour Town
is found in udon!

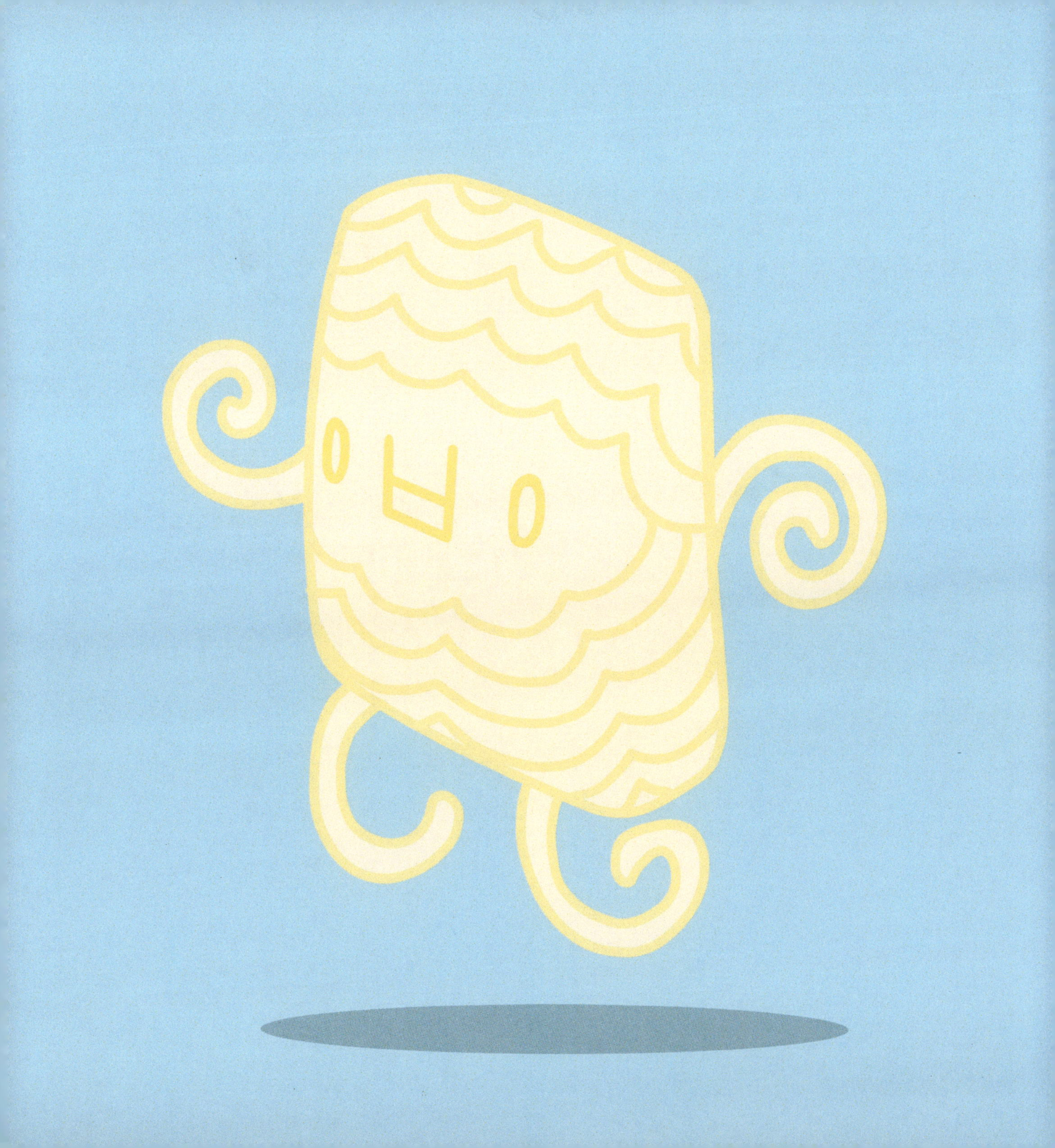

V is for vermicelli!

The Birth of Venus,
Botticelli!
The death of my Belt,
Vermicelli!

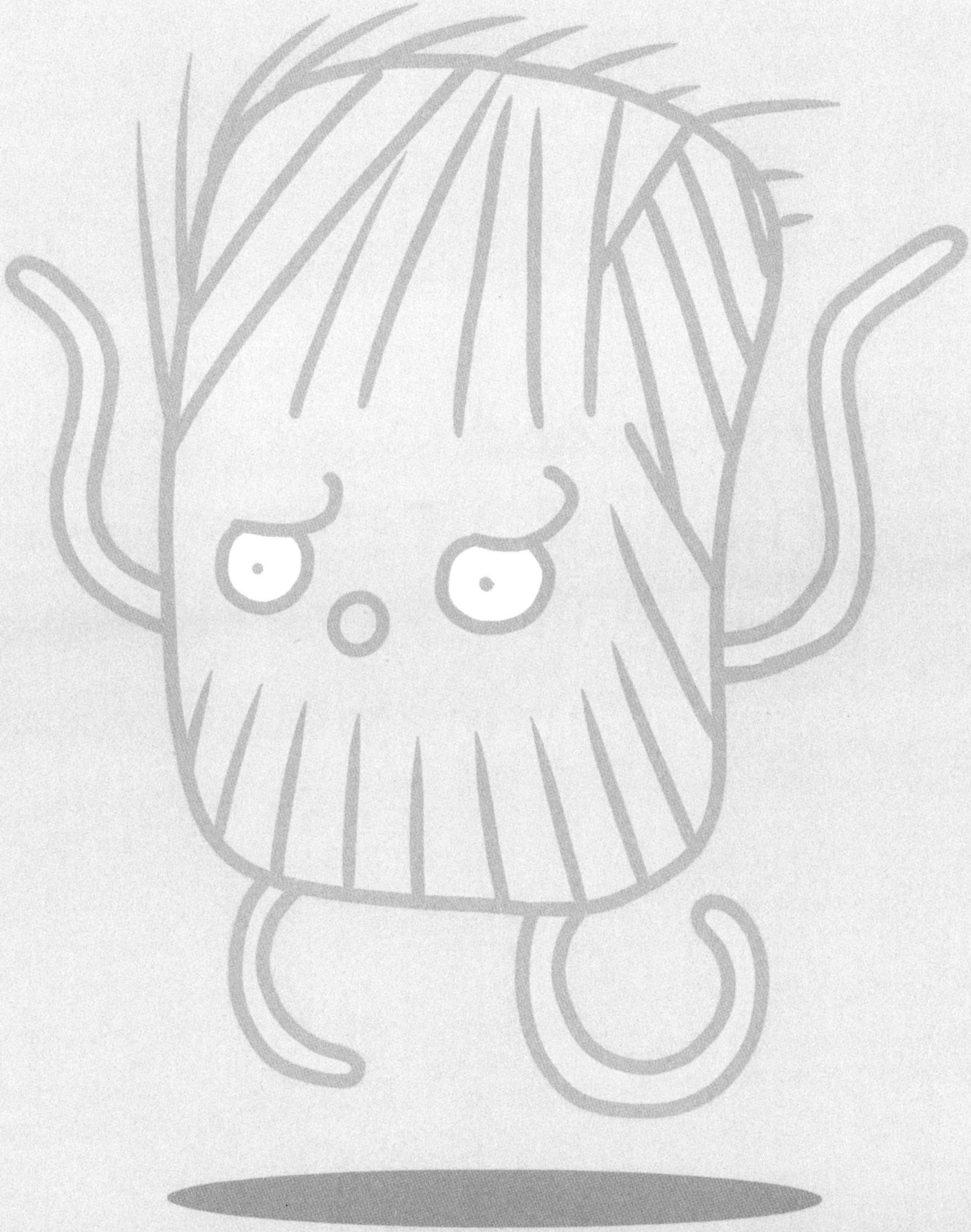

W is for winter melon!

If loving food is a crime, then I'm a felon! Deeply in love with winter melon!

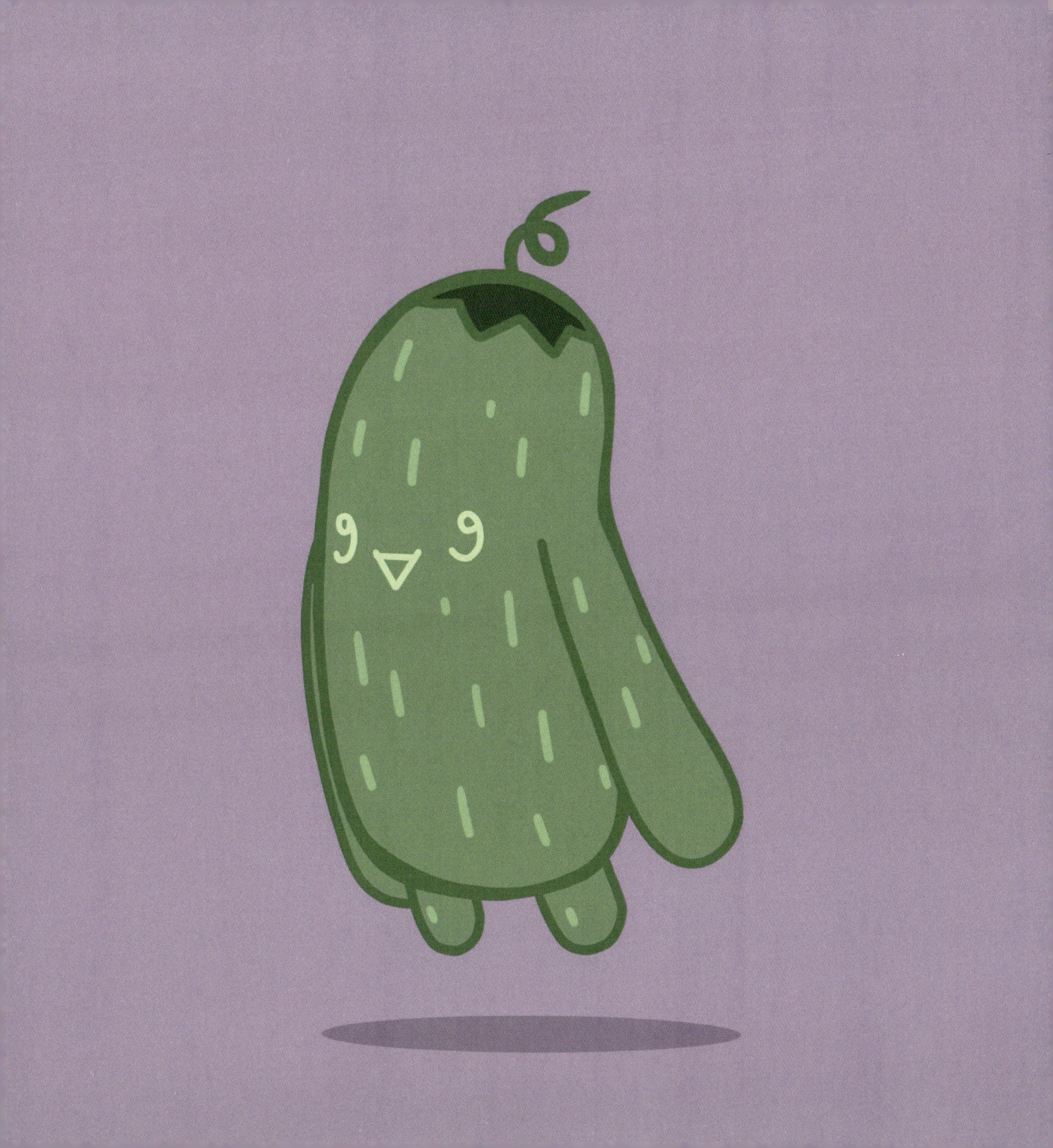

X is for XO!

XO sauce,
a little absurd.
I couldn't think
of another "X" word

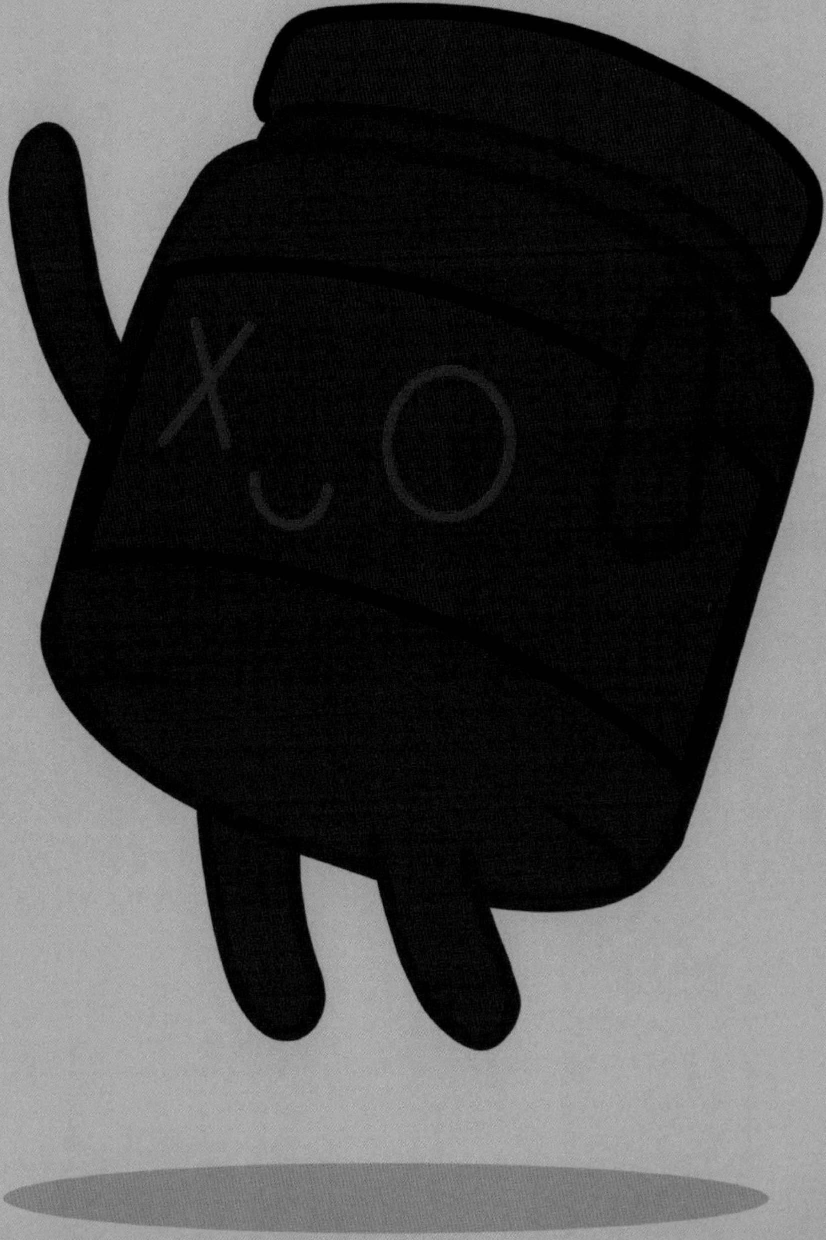

Y is for yam!

Confident?
Yes I am!
Delicious?
Yes I Yam!

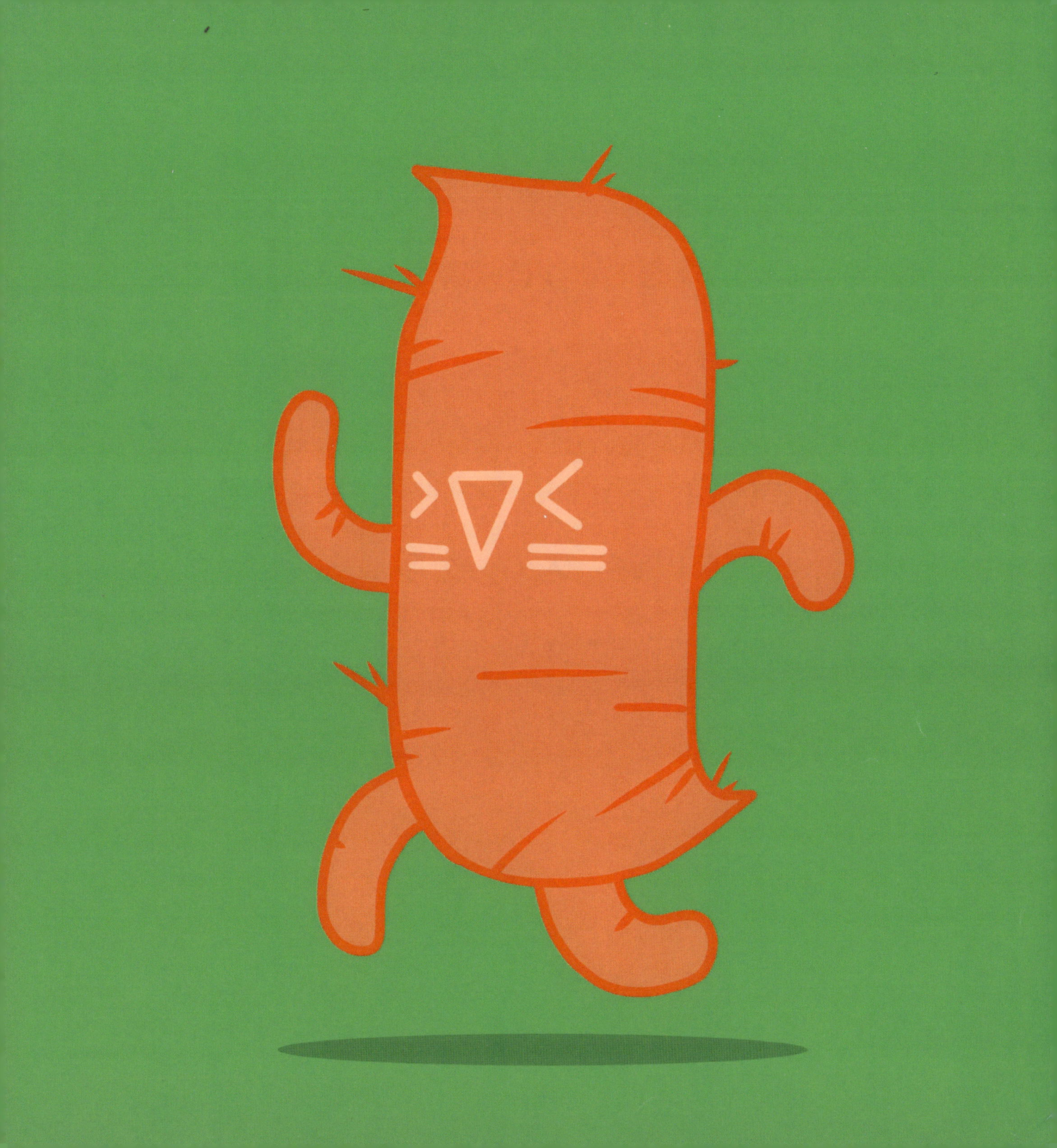

Z is for Zenith!

Never seen leftovers,
it's a myth.
If you see extra food,
invite Zenith!

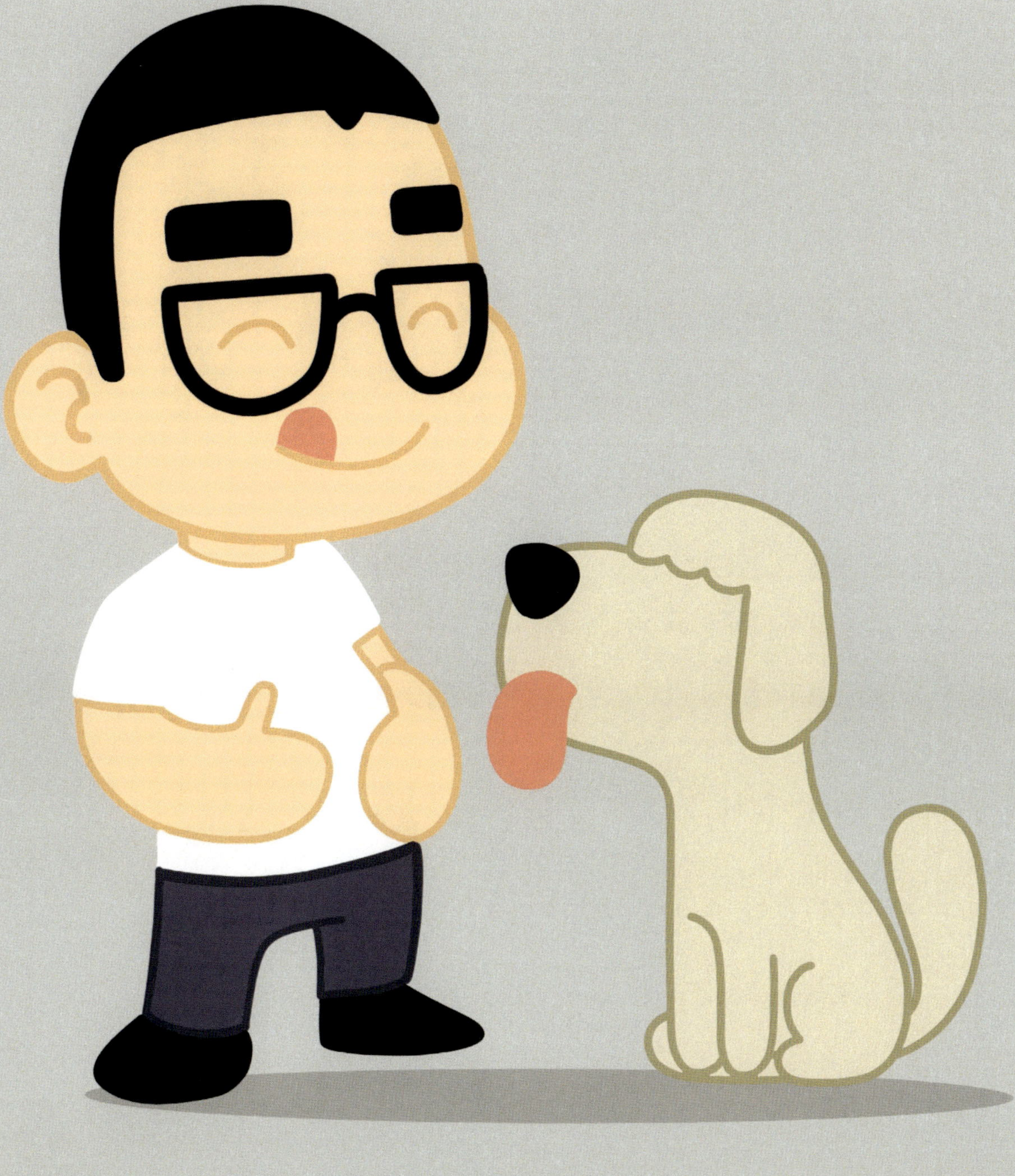

This book is dedicated to my wife and indigenous families that was on my heart during the making of this book.

Manufactured by Amazon.ca
Bolton, ON